TRAIN WINDOWS

David Allan Evans

Train Windows

Ohio University Press

Acknowledgements

The author and the publisher gratefully acknowledge permission to reprint the following poems which originally appeared in these magazines: "A Dream," "For a Pressman," *Back Door*; "Poet," *Crazy Horse*; "Pole Vaulter," "15 Years Later," *Esquire*; "Among Athletes," *The Far Point*; "Football," "After the Ten-Year Class Reunion," *Kansas Quarterly*; "Bus Station: 2 A.M.," *Midwest Quarterly*; "The Touchdown in Slow Motion," *Monmouth Review*; "After Play, Walking Home, Throwing Things Up at the Bats in the Darkening Sky," *North American Review*; "The Citizens' Complaint," "Some Lines After the Razing of the Sioux City Armour's Plant," *The New York Times*; "The Cattle Ghosts," "Deer on Cars," *Poetry Northwest*; "The Day My Uncle Made Everybody Look Up," "A Dream of Comforting," "The Story of Lava," "Feeding the Bears," "Tom Lonehill (1940-1956)," "In the Cemetery," *Poetry Now*; "Ford Pickup," "Old Man Driving in a Blizzard," *Prairie Schooner*; "Neighbors," "Watching Tackles in Slow Motion," "David's Tent," "The Blue Vase," "A Jumper," "Bus Depot Reunion," "The Bull Rider's Advice," "Train Windows," "Will You Sign My Brand-New Baseball, Louie?," *Shenandoah*; "Poem Without a Metaphor," "Winter-Kill," "Sunset," *South Dakota Review*; "Family Album," *Sou'-wester.*

"Sixteen Lines for a Sunday" appeared originally in *I Love You All Day It Is That Simple* (Abbey Press).

Compiled with the help of a 1974 fellowship grant from the National Endowment for the Arts.

for Jan,
and for Shelly,
David, and Kari

CONTENTS

Part I

Pole Vaulter

The approach to the bar
is everything

unless I have counted
my steps   hit my markers
feel up to it   I refuse
to follow through
I am committed to beginnings
or to nothing

planting the pole
at runway's end
jolts me
out of sprinting
I take off   kicking in
and up   my whole weight
trying the frailty
of fiberglass

never forcing myself
trusting it is right
to be taken to the end
of tension   poised for
the powerful thrust to
fly me beyond expectation

near the peak
I roll my thighs inward
arch my back   clearing
as much of the bar as I can
(knowing the best jump
can be cancelled
by a careless elbow)

and open my hands

The Citizens' Complaint

(Sioux City, 1972)

on their highest bluff
War Eagle's tomb
is eroding
knuckle by knuckle

into the Missouri

so they complain
call it unsightly

now there is talk
of the skull
visible all spring
impervious
even to flash floods

how do they explain
this thing? — —

this enemy among them
gazing down on the city
with eyes full of rain
who will not fall

into the river

Some Lines After the Razing of the
Sioux City Armour's Plant

it is 5 A.M. everything is the same as it was
the moon-hammered faces of the cattle are waiting
the line at the hiring gate is growing minute by minute
you can see the faces of yesterday or last year
or forty years ago looking more eager than they are
the same hands hiding out in the same pockets
if you wait long enough the gate will open up
inside everything will be the same as it always was
you will see knives glittering like the Missouri
pulleys ribs barrels guts tanks bones chopping blocks
any tooth could tell you the same old story
any hide if you had the time to listen

Whiteface Cattle Dying in a Blizzard

As the routine trails
they had been following
all morning gradually
whited out under them
and they began to drift,
they recalled in their
freezing held-up heads
a declining, a rising
something like

easing into water up to
their dripping chins and
heading out, trusting by
half-floating half-walking
the green opposite bank
will come across to them
and roll below their reborn
legs raising them up, up and
over letting them finally
one by one down onto a
different pasture.

Interstate 29

the white dog
suddenly
just up ahead
on the blacktop
shoulder was
looking
into the traffic
for a casual gap
then sauntered
onto the freeway
making me swerve
but tick him
going by then
in my rear-view
mirror he
gyrated back to
the blacktop
landing somehow
upright
shook himself out
and gazed in
my direction
growing
smaller and
smaller

The Bull Rider's Advice

what I'm saying is
you can't take this thing light
and there's no saddle to sit in

you can do it one of two ways
as far as I'm concerned
if you want to do it

you can get on just for the ride
take hold of the rope like it was
any old rope and pray for a quick 8 seconds
and no spinning

or you can wrap your fist into his back
so deep he knows you plan to stay awhile
dig in with your whole soul
until the sonofabitch is sick of you
and lets up

what I'm saying is
it's up to you

After Play, Walking Home, Throwing Things
Up at the Bats in the Darkening Sky

gripping the air,
blackly they screamed, the bats
bending his hat back on him

a baseball glove rose, *his* glove,
a hand flying out of his hand

the firefly eyes of the vacant lot
seeing his hand rise,
the bats falling up

the bats remember:
a hand went from him,

falling

Feeding the Bears

when
some day at
feeding time the
Grizzly
springs up over his wall

catch the
look
on the face of
the man who feeds
the animals

Winter-Kill

Long ears aim upwind.
December sun is
frozen in his eye.
He is hunched in the
last north acre
of the final field
where little game trails
cross and cross.

Someone is moving near
crouched   goggled
full tilt in the
Polar Cat - -

He whirls to go
but the Cat
is *here above him*
with him   silvering
over blurring stubble
until his breath
bursts like a torch
and he runs down slow inside
giving a face to snow
giving   into it.

Bullfrogs

For Ernie, Larry, and Bob

sipping a Schlitz
we cut off the legs,
packed them in ice, then
shucked the rest back into
the pond for turtles

ready to go home
we looked down and saw
what we had thrown back in:
quiet-bulging eyes nudging along
the moss's edge, looking up at us,

asking for their legs

Poet

that little
deaf man
and his iron-
wheeled cart
crunching
through the
cindered alleys
at odd hours
selecting
(before
the garbage truck
comes)
his useful
fabulous
junk

Deer on Cars

deer on cars
on the freeways
move with an ease
and speed and courage
that seem beyond them:
when diesels scream by
they may jiggle
but it's never a leap
in a new direction
and more often
it is they
that pass the diesels . . .

entering a city
the head settles down
as they ease up in school zones
halt at red lights
or go on green
staring straight ahead
in the proper lane

Ford Pickup

call me the Valiant heading west on Fourteen into the frozen
Dakota January sun and the one suddenly ahead the red
Custom Ranger with Texas plates and his woman taking
their time and all of my eye as he sits straight and tall
beneath a white Stetson nodding politely over frost heave
and she has my long my black my favorite hair with a ribbon
exactly the color of the pickup and feeling the cab's air
and now she scoots his way and lays her head on his shoulder
while he adjusts his hat and sways briefly over the yellow line
so then as they talk her hands are a bird's nest in her lap
to which the knuckles of his loose right hand are always returning

Lovers in the Car Wash

He took a left out of ordinary
traffic. They preferred to be
in the car while the machine,
for two quarters, washed it.
His hands stayed on the wheel;
the key was turned off.
Then the red and white brush
started up, then roaring swept
across the hood toward them. . .

What else could they do tonight or
this new spring more interesting?
Sitting perfect inside their
car-shaped storm rolling its
waters and colors forward and
backward over them - - his grip
whitening on the wheel,
her eyes, inside the streaming
glass, like sunflowers.

Bus Depot Reunion

just over the edge
of my *Life* a young sailor
bounds from a Greyhound's
hiss into his mother's hug,
steps back, trades hands
with his father, then turns
to an old, hunched man
maybe his grandfather - -

no hand, no word goes out,
they regard each other,

waiting for something, and
now their hands cup,

they begin to crouch
and spar, the old man

coming on like a pro,
snuffling, weaving,

circling, flicks
out a hook like a lizard's tongue,

the boy ducking, countering,
moving with his moves,

biffing at the bobbing
yellow grin, the clever

head, never landing a real
punch, never taking one

until suddenly, exactly
together they quit,

throw an arm around each other
and walk away laughing

17

Bus Station 2 A.M.

knuckling tne hissmg
strange light from her eyes
an old lady leans on
the bus driver's routine
hand, stepping hard down
into Hagerstown, Marylana
where her suitcase is
taken by a middle-aged man
who says *how are you*
almost touching her

he turns around
to lead her away
while she is nodding
and their faces reveal
mother and son

then they walk by me
and beyond
the suitcase drifting in
the gap between them

Neighbors

They live alone
together,

she with her wide hind
and bird face,
he with his hung belly
and crewcut.

They never talk
but keep busy.

Today they are
washing windows
(each window together)
she on the inside,
he on the outside.
He squirts Windex
at her face,
she squirts Windex
at his face.

Now they are waving
to each other
with rags,

not smiling.

Old Man Driving in a Blizzard

where snow is above
and ice is below

the less you see
the more you feel

THUMP THUMP
is something alive

but this in the chest
is *slow down slow down*

the left hand freezes
the right hand pulls

he begins at the edge
of concrete

a long descending
into snow

the doors sealed shut
no way to get back

from the air his
astonished breath

A Jumper

for Thomas James White Hawk, condemned to the electric chair

> *He held the state high*
> *school pole vault record*
> *of 13 feet, 7 ½ inches in*
> *1965.*
> *— from the* Minneapolis Star

We shall not let him
float out through the bars
in the odor of pea soup
     but
fit in the cage of his fingers
the warden's golden
curtain rod
and unlock the air of
the concrete yard for the
seconds
to a last vault:

who will ever hear
ever see him
moving in the moccasined dark
toward the law's
wall   that *this time* will
not bend him down who
bursts the inevitable
jolt   steals up
his loins
learns
too late his name?

In a Wheelchair, in a Nursing Home

the toes
of her bright black shoes
click
to the habit
of a frail tune
on a frail breath

did you ever see a lassie
a lassie
a lassie

while silence
waits in her hands
that wait in her lap
that is silent

The Day Bud Abbott Died

Today Bud Abbott is dead,
whose skinny face I bumped into
last month on a magazine cover
in a checkout line at the A&P.
All over America the cash registers
were ringing up Bud Abbott's face.

But today Bud Abbott is dead.

Let cash registers keep on ringing it up for Bud Abbott!

Ring up THE DAY BUD ABBOTT DIED!
Ring up APRIL 24th, 1974!
Ring up AT THE AGE OF 78!
Ring up LOU COSTELLO DIED IN 1959!

Keep on ringing it up for Bud Abbott!

Ring up the Wolf Man's box of Wheaties!
Ring up his spittled teeth and his face that can't help it!
Ring up his diffident hardon too!
Ring up Dr. Jekyll's frozen TV dinner!
Ring up Mr. Hyde's Purina Puppy Chow!
Ring up the Invisible Man's Loaf of Wonder Bread dancing in mid-air
above the counter!
Ring up the zippered forehead of Glenn Strange!
Ring up his stiff limp and his orthopedic shoes and his Disney grin!
Ring up the candle sliding across the rising casket lid!
Ring up the funny fear on the fat man's face as he watches it!
Ring up WHOSE ON FIRST a million times!
Ring up WHAT'S ON THIRD a million more times!
Ring up cash registers laughing their heads off all over America
for the death of Bud Abbott!

Tom Lonehill (1940-1956)

Opposed to crewcuts and buddies,
his black hair slick as grackles,
his black belt silver studded,
Tom Lonehill hid on his porch all day
behind thick eyebrows watching us.

He saw nothing good about slamming
a bamboo pole into a box and clearing
a ten-foot bar and falling back
down into heaped sawdust;
or smacking a baseball on the roof
of Woodrow Wilson Junior High;
or place-kicking a football over
a sagging telephone wire;
or shuffling spread-legged and
holding a beam of light underground
through the cool sewers of summer.

The rest of us made it, taking
a diploma, a wife, and a job and
settling down as our fathers before.
Now we tell our sons about baseball
and football and falling back into
sawdust and steering a beam of light
through the blind sewers.

But none of us explain Tom Lonehill - -
how he hid on his porch all day behind
his eyebrows, how in the county jail
leaping from his cot he hanged himself
with his belt in the middle of a night
in July in the middle of his 16th summer.

For Pete, for the Summer
We Tore up 20 Miles of Abandoned
Rock Island Track Near Promise City, Iowa

(1)

With hands gone soft
and 15 years away
I keep an eye on you yet,
up in that red crane's
window framing your teethy
grin and the pipe stuck in it
forever. That boom is swaying,
those bright tongs are hovering,
so all I can do is
reach up as they drop
down through the patient
afternoon and let them settle
easy and light as pigeons
into my leather hands, then
clamp a loosened rail,
lift my thumb and rise
with the load just so high,
leap off and get set
for them again and again - -
all this in a single motion
that goes on even after
the others have gone home,
the pay has stopped, and the rusty
dark is here.

(2)

The job and Promise City
dead, and the last paychecks
in our pockets, we hitched a ride
on a flatbed truck heading
north on Interstate 20 - -
your words shouted between bursts
of pipe smoke in the wind
until you coiled up and slept
on a heap of work clothes - -
while I watched the new
green cornfields rise and
fall around us and away
yet come again, again
constant as ticking frost heave
or meadow larks' songs leaping
from fence post to powerline
ahead, behind, on all sides
that day the sun was
tracing on the blue dome
of August its own certain line . . .

you woke up 10 miles out
of Sioux City and all the way in
bragged how you'd kill a pint
of Old Crow and take on
that 200-pound redheaded
whore at the Swan Hotel
on lower Fourth.

Watching Tackles in Slow Motion

I key on anything that moves. —*Deacon Jones*

Up floats the turf   the shark is rising
    the slow hawk
               bends the air
tooth and talon
    touch where he moves exactly out of
certain as a polar bear
come from a death
             in the jawed and frozen green
saying
I will always find you   always find you.

Football

Consider the stoning of beasts:
the peppered mammoth slobbering in the pit,
the stunned boar,
the bear with crushed face advancing,
the crippled skirling cat;

consider the hands
groping along the hacked shores of rivers
how many dawns ago? for this shape of stone.

"Will You Sign My Brand-New Baseball, Louie?"

the best thing in my head
of baseball and Kansas City
is the Royals playing the
Red Sox and the drunk trying
to get Louie Aparicio
to sign his brand-new baseball:
every time Louie comes loping in
from shortstop at the end
of the half inning there he is
the drunk elbowing his way
from high up in the grandstand
down into the box seats and all
those turned-around wrinkled
foreheads and goddammits and
uplifted cups of Hamms and
Dr. Pepper with amazing
timing to catch his man
exactly at the screen except
that Louie every time
fields with his eyes that
white routine ball coming
out of the crowd and drops
his look and speeds up just
a little then disappears
into the dugout safe as the
fans cheer and cheer and
cheer for both of their heroes

Part II

Train Windows

one night I am standing
on a high bluff
overlooking the tracks
waiting for him to leave
once and for all time

suddenly I see his face
in each lighted window
of his train - - the face
of a man passing
from darkness into darkness
reading a novel

as I leap I snatch a
white pigeon from the air
and wave with that same hand
going down to my father

15 Years Later

driving by the house I see her alone
watering the grass
in pin curls and white shorts
purple rivers on her legs

where are the six kids?
the husband?

not wanting to be seen I
speed up but honk in case she noticed - -

out of the rear-view mirror
she looks into my life
waving

The Touchdown in Slow Motion

The way to turn thirty
Is to kill off the light
And begin over
In slow motion:

So here I go
   in the shape
of my father's hope
   on a 30 sweep right
ranging out   cutting
   now turning it on
turning the corner
   to give up turf and
snatch what I
   need to be nifty
with a last fake
   in a farewell wave of my hand

stretching out
   I find my light
and a way to move
   in the green world

After the Ten-Year Class Reunion

I'm floating 72 yards
down these stairs untouched

O Ward Vosburg   my pulling
left guard   is that your

helmet or head
below me shining

with the tall eyes
of stadium lights?

protect me   show me
the Way   hold up

your trophy for the most
pounds gained in 10 years

you never needed
for killing all sport coats

crowding the 5 hole - -
Vosy   what is there

next   after the last
good fake on the last

step   after the cheers
the retiring of my golden

Blazer by Weatherwax   size 44
what is there

for this old halfback palming
the seam of a can of Hamms?

Among Athletes

I stand of this track.

Two runners come near into my air.

   They smell like sweat clothes.
   I smell like Jade East cologne.

   They are not thinking much.
   I am thinking much.

(I am thinking they are running circles around me and
my head may swim into their circles.

   Soon they will leave on light legs.

A Poem on the Changing of Wall Street into Floyd Boulevard in My Hometown, Sioux City

driving up the
street that used
to stop 20
years ago at
Alan Cooley's house
no longer there
on the edge
of a bluff
a street that
now breaks out
over the city
into a convenient
boulevard that goes
right by the
only brick house
on Wall and
white picket fence
where I grew
up suddenly I
am a man
who won't be
stopping here again
a man always
going by

For a Pressman

what has become
of those ink-stained hands
Father - -

those fading maps
of strange countries
I never got to?

The Blue Vase

for my sister (1930-1969)

It may be as a thief
or father of daughters
but 'most nights still.
on my way to sleep
I must get through my sister's
bedroom, not waking
the one who went to bed early,

and fall on the odors
of her dresser and secret
blue vase,
hushed to the tiptoes,
contenting my hands
with trinkets:

the glass sea horse
drowned in Crackerjacks,
the Indian Head penny
losing face, a couple
of dogs, black and white,
magnetically stuck
on each other.

It may be some night
my sister will be too deep
in sleep for the hands
of thief or brother
to wake her, or the vase
will be empty.

In the Cemetery

I came here
assuming
you were
close to

the statue of Mary

but now
I can't
tell your grave
from the others

Granny

that little room
you lived in - -
how its things, its odors
never forget me!

those cheap, heated-over
porkchops, jars of Vicks,
keys, Indian Head pennies,
balls of string, Smith Bros.
Cherry Cough Drops, those
dilapidated, felt slippers

and that one bare bulb
hanging from the ceiling - -
how it keeps my whole
childhood lit!

Family Album

I have you, Father, in that photo where
you stand in the middle of one of your last
live summers between two ripening girls
in bathing suits (the one I would marry,
and her friend), your arms entirely framing
their shoulders. You look happy, comfortable,
as though you could hold up that scene forever.
Your sunny smile is not just for whoever is
aiming the camera; it is for my future wife,
as it should be. Everything looks complete - -

except your hands that flare out from
the bare shoulders' feminine roundness,
that place where cupped male hands often
fill themselves. Not these, they want to fly
off somewhere to be alone with their huge
fear, or, diffident and powerful as they are,
they want to carry all three of you away
completely out of the picture.

The Cattle Ghosts

(Sioux City: I am standing where Armour's used to be)

Where they came from once
they come from yet:
a place far off and quieter
for its few swallows
and peeled, face-sunken barns

in the spittled wombs of trucks
through Iowa's screaming nights
they come head on

to this louder land
of the kick and prod
and hammered breath

dying is a shy habit here
that goes on always:
the one with the face of a friend
the one with the mushroomed eye
the one with the limp

I am near them all
though the kill-floor heavens fall

David's Tent

because
    the army blanket over the clothesline
    became
suddenly
    a tent tonight

just by shadows

son
    I want to tell you   my father
    should not be
a shadow
          in the ground

The Second Day of Winter, 1972

I live in Brookings, South Dakota where it is cold
and windy this time of year but it is unusually warm
for the second day of winter the sun in the tall pines
that I walked under this morning on my way to work
and that I will walk under this evening on my way home
a girl named Brenda her boots the color of wet brown
a four-page letter from a good friend in Washington
with a plan for going after steelhead next summer in Alaska
nobody expects snow the weatherman expects a blue sky
there can be wind in December the empty streets can fill up
with empty garbage cans after the men have dumped them
but today there is no wind and nobody expects any wind
it is unusually warm for the second day of winter
there is no snow no wind no suffering and no death

A Dream of Comforting

a young man skiing
down a hill falls suddenly
tumbling into a
crowd lighting
beside a fence
one leg ripped off

many try to help
but he climbs over the snow
along the fence
to be alone

I walk into the crowd
bend down and circle
his chest with my arms
and lean him against me
to tell his blue eyes
he will be all right

he lets go of himself
I comfort him
until the ambulance comes
to take him away

The Day My Uncle Made Everybody Look Up

One Thanksgiving
with everybody there
soon after the blessing
(said by him as usual)
his Pure Blooded
Blue Mountain Shepherd
standing by the table
barked for no reason
and he told him in a calm voice
to calm down
but the dog kept it up
and he said again
even calmer than before
to calm down or else
so when the dog kept it up
he neatly folded his napkin
beside his plate
excused himself
got up and went to the den
came back with his Double Barrelled
Remington Twelve Gauge
aimed it carefully at the dog
blasted twice
discharged the cartridges
took the gun back to the den
came back and sat down
placed his napkin on his lap
and said please pass the potatoes.

My Dream

I'm working on the dock at Armour's in line pulling my cart with the others. We're loading loins into a box car that will go east. But the man in front of me is pulling a tankage cart with two old men in it, dressed in black suits. Their backs are to me. The line stops. Everybody notices the old men. One sits still, looking down, maybe at his hands. The other is mumbling, holding up a syringe and waving it in the air. I hear him say he is 112 years old. Another man walks up to the cart. He is wearing a white frock and has a big silver badge that says "Federal Inspector." He says to the old man with the syringe: "Are you sure you want to go through with it?" The old man nods his head. The man in white nods back. The old man stands up in the cart, turns around facing me, then puts the syringe to his shoulder. He just stands there. Then he grows taller. Also he looks proud. His face wrinkles in pain, he falls back dead into the cart. The line begins to move again. The man that is still alive looks straight ahead.

Sunset

Before I left my spot
on a bridge over the Sioux
watching the sun go down,
I heaved a single handful
of gravel that, when it

met the silent current
burst into applause

Poem Without a Metaphor

for Father, dead seven springs

the seventh robin
lights on the thumb
of my son

my lilac bush
is doing its
white explosions

a south breeze
stirs my unnamed tree

the Missouri
swells far from the
bluff of your grave

a Dakota farmer
inverts a corn field

a rock
will soon go skimming
the perfectly round
pond of childhood:

seven springs
and still I lack
the metaphor
of your death

Sixteen Lines for a Sunday

How shall I earn my bread?

Jogging?
Hung with heavy togs and belly,
One mile, to return where I began?
And still the doctor and a tired heart
Will go unpleased.

Learning?
A few pages I might read
To learn what I cannot read.

Napping?
It is too early for the grave davenport.

But one wise thought I will touch to fullness:
Bribing the children
With what shiny coins are left,
I will fasten all locks, draw all curtains,
And take my woman to bed.

What is Said

all those times I
have come into you and
will come into you again
and again and all those times you
have come and
will come again and again
are all the times we
add against the time
we will lie no longer
together

this is what is said
when I come into you and
this is what is said
when you come

Rainbow

for David

all morning snaking
down through aspen
with a stream
and a new sun
you and I crept
now and then on
all fours secretly
opened the stiff weeds
flicked a red worm on the ripples
dazzled five trout
for your shouldered creel

until we found a spot
where the stream deepened
to a hole and a thing
in it   hovering
that refused our lures
and underwater hands
but stayed us
a quick hour to watch it
change over and over

shadow into
pink current into
shadow into pink
current into
shadow

Looking Out My Bedroom Window at 3 A.M.

I am trees, you are wind:
Make me speak and sway.

The Story of Lava

Every time I smell Lava soap it is 1948.
My father is bending over a long sink in the
pressroom of *The Sioux City Journal* at 5 A.M.,
his grey long-underwear peeled down over his
white belly, a thin bar of Lava tumbling over
and over slowly in his ink-stained hands.
The morning news has passed through his hands
out into the morning streets into the hands
of sleepy boys who fold it a certain way and
fling it on porches and steps, but that is not
my story. Lava is my story and the morning
news that Lava can't rub off. It is my father
bending over a sink, a thin bar of Lava tumbling
over and over and over slowly in his cloudy hands.